EVERYDAY HEROES
Of The Heart

By Jill C. Wheeler

Published by Abdo & Daughters, 4940 Viking Drive, Suite 622, Edina, Minnesota 55435.

Printed in the United States.

Edited by Julie Berg

Library of Congress Cataloging-in-Publication Data

Wheeler, Jill C., 1964-
    Everyday Heroes of the Heart / Jill C. Wheeler
     p. cm. -- (Everyday Heroes)
    Includes index.
    Summary: Tells the stories of five young people who volunteer in a variety of activities to help others.
    ISBN 1-56239-701-X
    1. Voluntarism--United States--Case studies--Juvenile literature. 2. Volunteers--United States--Case studies--Juvenile literature. 3.Youth volunteers in social service--United States--Juvenile literature. 4.Youth volunteers in community development--United States--Case studies--Juvenile literature. [1. Voluntarism.] I. Title.
    HN90.V64W49 1996   96-7356
    302'.14--dc20   CIP
                                     AC

Contents

The Greatest Gift of All

Traci Taylor spent a lot of time in the hospital as a child. She still remembers how volunteers at the hospital would come by with a special cart loaded with craft projects.

Traci began to look forward to seeing the cart and choosing a project to work on. The crafts helped ease the loneliness and pain of endless days in the hospital. Today, Traci has changed roles. Now she's the one walking the halls of the hospital bringing relief to young patients.

Traci is one of more than 105 million Americans who volunteer each year. About eight million of these volunteers are between the ages of 14 and 17. They and other volunteers spend an average of four hours per week helping others. If their organizations had to pay them, the time these volunteers spend would be worth more than $174 billion dollars.

In the following chapters, you'll read stories about some of these amazing young people. These are stories of love and courage. Of balancing school work and volunteer work. Of making a difference in people's lives. Of making a difference in their own lives.

You'll also see how by reaching out to help others, these young people also are reaching inward. They are Heroes of the Heart.

Everyone has the power to make a difference. It doesn't matter how old you are. It doesn't matter where you live. At the end of the book, you'll even find ideas on what you can do. If everyone pitches in, the world will be a much better place.

Traci Taylor

Traci Taylor was only six years old when doctors told her she had leukemia. She spent much of the next three years in hospitals. Those days were often long and lonely. While in a hospital in Dallas, Texas, Traci found something to look forward to. It was a craft cart that volunteers brought around to patients. Traci would pick out projects that would make the days pass quicker.

While Traci was still sick she moved with her family to a smaller town with a smaller hospital. That hospital had a special playroom for very young patients. However, there was nothing for older kids like Traci.

Traci never forgot that. When she was 10, she received a bone-marrow transplant. That transplant cured her cancer. Then she decided it was time to do something to help patients back in her hometown hospital in Cape Girardeau, Missouri.

Together with her father, her brother and people from her church, Traci built a special cart. The red, wooden cart is shaped like a train. It's filled with toys. One evening after school each week, Traci pushes the cart around the hospital. She hands out toys, books and crafts to young patients. She also does other volunteer work at the hospital. She says she's willing to help out wherever people need her.

Traci Taylor, winner of the Maxwell House Real Heroes Award.

Traci's work hasn't gone unnoticed. Her mother nominated her for the Maxwell House Real Heroes Awards Program. Judges in the program picked Traci as one of 50 real heroes. She flew to Washington, D.C., and met former First Lady, Barbara Bush. Many organizations around Cape Girardeau also have recognized Traci for her work.

"It's important to give back when people give to you," Traci says of her work. "I think of all the help I received when I was in the hospital. Now I can give that help back to the kids who are in the hospital today."

Traci hopes to pursue a career in the medical field when she graduates from school. In the meantime, her work at the hospital is giving her practical experience. It's also reminding her of the importance of sticking with a goal — despite problems. "Any dreams that you have can come true if you just keep on trying," she advises. "Don't ever give up. It will all work out."

It's important
to give back.

Nick Snavely

Few people are lucky enough to have a huge nature preserve in their backyard. Nick Snavely of Dayton, Minnesota, does. It's part of the reason he's so passionate about nature. It's also why he's spent more than 600 hours helping others enjoy nature, too.

Nick is a volunteer with the local parks system. He does everything from cleaning animal cages to reading to young park visitors. He also loves to teach others about nature.

In 1995, the parks system named him a distinguished volunteer. He was one of only six people to receive the award. More than 700 people volunteer for the parks system. Nick takes the honor in stride.

"The most rewarding part of volunteering is sharing knowledge," he says. "There are so many things out there to know, and you wish most people knew them, but they don't. That's why you want to share your knowledge with others."

Nick first got involved with the parks system when he was just 10 years old. He attended a nature class. The class hooked him. Now he teaches those classes. The classes instruct people how important nature is and shows them how to protect it. Nick can spend up to 30 hours a week teaching and volunteering.

Nick Snavely, a distinguished volunteer.

Teaching is important to Nick. He advises everyone to continue learning — no matter how old they are. "The more you learn, the better," he says. "Anything you learn will help you out later in life." Sometimes Nick teaches with a naturalist who works for the parks system. "I usually learn a lot, too," he says of his co-teacher.

Nick's dedication has earned him many friends. Some of the people who work for the parks system think of him as a co-worker. Nick even attends meetings of the local city council. He likes to stay informed of decisions the council makes. Some of those decisions affect the nature preserve. Despite the time he spends volunteering, Nick also makes sure he has time to study.

Nick is a sophomore in high school. After graduation, he plans to go to college to study biology. Someday he would like to be a naturalist.

"If you haven't experienced nature and wildlife, then you don't understand what it's about," he adds. "It's so much fun to be out in the parks doing stuff, working with people, showing them things in nature."

Share your knowledge with others.

Pia Cruz

Pia Cruz and her family moved to North Hills, California, from their native Philippines to find a better life. Once they arrived, the Cruz family quickly began making life better for everyone else, too.

Youth Services encourages young people to volunteer and get involved in the community. Under Pia's leadership, local youth got busy. They did beach clean-ups, park clean-ups and worked with other community service groups.

Pia also helped the local Red Cross chapter organize a Trash-A-Thon fundraiser. Volunteers collected trash from around the city and signed up sponsors. Sponsors donated a set amount of money for each pound of trash collected. The event raised more than $2,000.

Additionally, Pia and her youth volunteers made the holidays brighter for some local residents. They collected gift donations from local stores, wrapped them and gave them to kids at a local children's home. At Halloween, they visited a veteran's hospital to give out bags of candy.

Opposite page:
Pia Cruz won the
J.C.Penney Golden
Rule Award.

Pia's work has earned her the J.C. Penney Golden Rule Award, the United Way Youth Leadership Award and designation as a Red Cross National Convention Alternate Youth Speaker. Her dedication also has earned her the respect of many adults. Some of them didn't think young people could be serious about helping others.

Pia now is studying business and biological science at Santa Monica College. She hopes to be a doctor someday and to continue helping others through the Red Cross.

"I'd like to expand into developing countries and have clinics all over to help people," she says. "I hear about what people's lives are like in those places. And I feel badly that I have as much as I do and they don't have that."

Pia also believes young people need to put their education to work for the good of others. "Integrity without knowledge is weak, but knowledge without integrity is even weaker," she says. "If you don't use your common sense along with facts and statistics, you won't be able to see the whole picture."

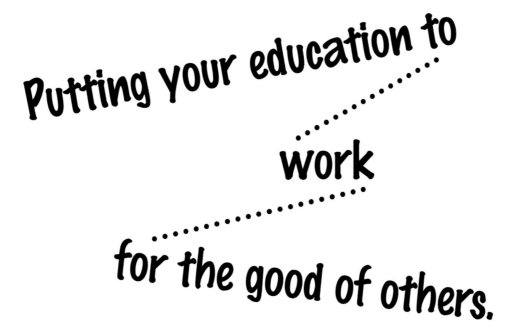

Putting your education to work for the good of others.

 # Russell Roberson

Russell Roberson was very shy as a child — so shy he even mumbled when he talked. "I felt like I was missing out on things," he remembers. "I didn't know as many people as others did."

He decided to do something about it by getting involved in the local Boys and Girls Club in his hometown of Little Rock, Arkansas. That changed everything. He took on leadership roles, gave speeches and began to give of himself. Since then, nothing's been the same.

Russell has devoted a lot of his spare time to helping others. He has tutored other young people. He helped put on a Halloween carnival for children in a disadvantaged neighborhood. He painted homes for people who couldn't do it themselves. He also worked on the "Service to Seniors" program keeping elderly citizens' apartments clean. Additionally, he started a bingo program for them.

Russell's work caught the attention of the Boys & Girls Club of America organization. In 1995, the group named him Southwest Regional Youth of the Year for his leadership and community service. His high school in Little Rock named him Student of the Year. He maintained a perfect grade point average there.

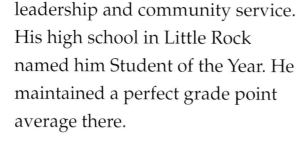

Russell Roberson received the Southwest Regional Youth of the Year Award.

Between volunteering, Russell enjoys golfing and playing music. He's now a freshman at Hendrix College in Conway, Arkansas. He is studying biology and chemistry to become a researcher or a doctor.

Russell is quick to advise other young people to get involved in their communities. "Being involved helped me realize I could do more than I thought," he said. "When I was little I always thought about being a doctor. But I'd talk myself out of it, saying it was too hard. Through being involved and getting recognition, I saw that I could do some things I didn't think I could."

"If you really want to do something, don't let someone tell you that you can't just because it's hard," he adds. "People exaggerate how hard things are. Often they're not that difficult. If you want to do something, just believe you can. If you work hard, you'll be able to accomplish it."

If you work hard you .... can accomplish it.

 # Shannon Selmon

Giving to others has been so much a part of Shannon Selmon's life that she can't imagine it any other way.

Shannon began her volunteer work in second grade. She helped her mother serve food and clean up at a local shelter that her mother had helped organize. They named it Food and Shelter for Friends.

"At the time I didn't think anything of it," she recalls. "But looking back, it showed me there are a lot of people less fortunate. Everyone needs to pitch in and help make a difference."

Shannon is always looking for opportunities to do just that. She listened to a singing group from Zambia, Africa, sing at her church. Afterwards, she got to know some of

the members. When she heard some of them needed suits
for a special reception in their home country, Shannon
bought two suits for them. She used money she'd earned
baby-sitting. She also helped set up concert dates for the
group at other schools in her hometown of Norman,
Oklahoma.

Shannon has helped people outside of her hometown as
well. She went on a mission trip to Costa Rica with a group
of people from her church. The volunteers built a church in
a village there and held a Bible school for the local children.
On the trip, she heard about a two-year-old boy who
needed a heart and liver transplant. When she returned to
the U.S., Shannon set about helping raise money for the boy.
It didn't matter to her that she'd never met him.

Shannon Selmon receiving the Young American Medal.

Her efforts have earned her two major awards. She received the Golden Rule Award from J.C. Penney for her work with Food and Shelter for Friends. She still volunteers at the shelter. She helps with meals, talks to clients and even organizes fundraisers. The United States Department of Justice also gave Shannon its 1993 Young American Medal for her volunteer work. Shannon flew to Washington, D.C., to receive the award in fall 1995.

Yet the awards are not the reason Shannon keeps on giving to others. She credits her faith with her strong desire to help. "All I can do is try to give back to people less fortunate," she says. "It feels good to give back to people."

She adds that young people shouldn't let their age stop them from lending a hand. "It doesn't matter how old you are. A lot of people will say you can't help, that you're too young. But it doesn't matter."

In addition to her volunteer work, Shannon plays basketball at the high school where she's a sophomore. After graduation, she hopes to continue playing basketball in college while studying criminal psychology.

She also hopes to keep up her volunteer work. For her, finding projects is never difficult. She encourages other young people to adopt the same attitude. "Whenever you see a problem, or someone who needs help, there's always something you can do. It doesn't matter how small it is."

It feels good to give back to people.

# How to Be A Hero

Young people are an important part of voluntarism. In fact, a national study by the Commission on Resources for Youth found that young people are the "largest, the most zestful and the most under-used manpower pool of all..." Some schools even require their students to volunteer or perform community service to graduate.

If you'd like to make a difference in someone else's life — and your own — consider volunteering. It's easy. It also can be fun. You can do it as little or as much as you like. Here are some ideas on how to get started.

First, decide what kind of volunteer work you'd like to do. Start by asking yourself what your interests and skills are. Do you enjoy doing arts and crafts? Do you enjoy sports? Reading? Are you good at visiting with people?

Next, find out what volunteer jobs will let you use the interests and skills you just identified. There are many, many volunteer opportunities out there. One is bound to be just right for you.

Remember, too, you're more likely to stick with your volunteer job if you feel strongly about the organization or cause. Do you believe hunger is a terrible problem? Then work toward helping people get enough to eat. Do you love animals? Consider volunteering with a humane society. Do you want to help people in an emergency? Consider volunteering with the American Red Cross.

There are several ways to get involved in volunteering. You can do it with a group, or do it on your own. Some groups that volunteer include church youth groups, Boy or Girl Scouts, or youth groups at the local YMCA. By joining these groups, you'll get a chance to participate in their volunteer projects.

There also are special clubs or school groups that do volunteer work. If your school requires community service work to graduate, there probably is a special office to help you find volunteer opportunities.

If you decide to volunteer on your own, you'll need to do a little extra research. Look in your local newspaper. Many newspapers carry a listing of volunteer opportunities. Look on community bulletin boards in stores and malls. Ask the clergy person at your church. If your family already volunteers, consider pitching in with them. Call the local office of the United Way. You can find the number in your local telephone book. Or, if you know the organization you want to help, give them a call.

The Internet can help you find volunteer opportunities, too. Visit the Impact Online World Wide Web site. It lists local agencies that match volunteers and non-profits. You can find it at http://www.webcom.com/~iol. Or, call the Points of Light Foundation 24 hours a day at 1-800-879-5400. The Foundation can help you find volunteer opportunities near you.

Once you've found a volunteer opportunity, treat it like a regular job. The organization may ask you to fill out an application. Some agencies also interview potential volunteers. They'll ask questions about your interests and backgrounds. They'll ask about your skills. Tell them about any special skills such as speaking another language. Knowledge of computers and working well with others also are valuable skills.

Remember that volunteering is a two-way street. Make sure you're interested in the job they have in mind for you. Also keep in mind hours and transportation. Will your volunteering interfere with your schoolwork? Can you get where you need to go by bicycle or bus?

When you begin volunteering, make sure you're on time. Show up when you're expected. Come prepared to do your job. Dress appropriately. When it comes time to apply for a job, don't forget the work you did as a volunteer, either. It can count as work experience.

Finally, enjoy the experience of volunteering. It's an excellent way to meet new people and make new friends. It's also a great way to make a difference.

GLOSSARY OF TERMS

cancer — a disease that causes cells to multiply too fast.

integrity — to stick to the things you believe in.

leukemia — a disease where white blood cells increase too fast.

naturalist — a person who studies nature.

preserve—an area restricted for protection and preservation of natural resources.

shelter—something that covers or affords protection.

transplant—to transfer an organ from one part of an individual to another.

veteran — someone who has served in the armed forces.

voluntarism—doing something by or relying on voluntary action.

Index